I CAN BE AN ANIMAL DOCTOR

By Kathryn Wentzel Lumley

Prepared under the direction of Robert Hillerich, Ph.D.

CHILDRENS PRESS®

CHICAGO

Library of Congress Cataloging in Publication Data

Lumley, Kathryn Wentzel.
  I can be an animal doctor.

  Includes index.
  Summary: A simple description of the work of a veterinarian
and the preparation necessary for a career in this field.
  1. Veterinarians—Juvenile literature. 2. Veterinary
medicine—Vocational guidance—Juvenile literature.
[1. Veterinarians. 2. Occupations] I. Title.
SF756.L86 1985   636.089'023   85-12802
ISBN 0-516-01836-1

PICTURE DICTIONARY

cages

nurse

veterinarian   examining room   lab assistant

animal hospital

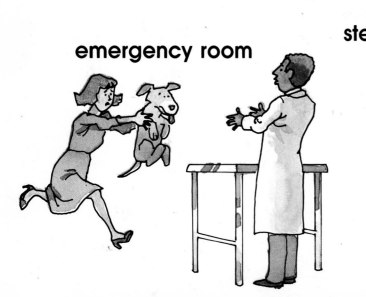

emergency room

thermometer

stethoscope

surgeon

nurse

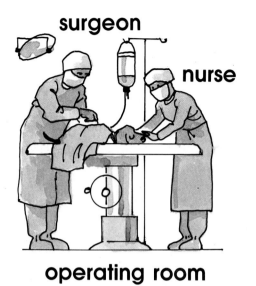

operating room

x ray

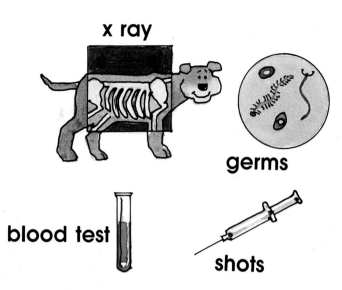

germs

blood test

shots

medicine

school

research

microscope

patients

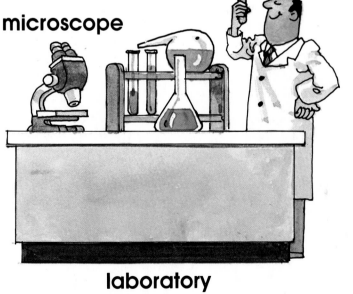

laboratory

Pet owners make sure that their pets have regular checkups.

Have you ever visited a
doctor's office where all
the patients were
animals?

Dogs, cats, birds, fish,
snakes, and maybe
rabbits wait side by side.
Do you think that they
talk with each other?

patients

A veterinarian carefully checks a cockatoo.

veterinarian

school

A doctor who treats animals is called a veterinarian. Men and women must go to school for a long time to become veterinarians. They must love animals and want to help them.

In school they learn
how to tell when animals
are sick. And, best of all,
they find out how to
make them well and
keep them that way.

Animals get sick just as
people do. They catch
cold, break bones, and
get hurt. But they can't
talk and tell the doctor
how they feel.

Without special instruments, vets could not learn why animals are sick.

A doctor has many
ways to find out why an
animal is sick.

Eyes and ears are
checked. The coat of an
animal with fur is
examined.

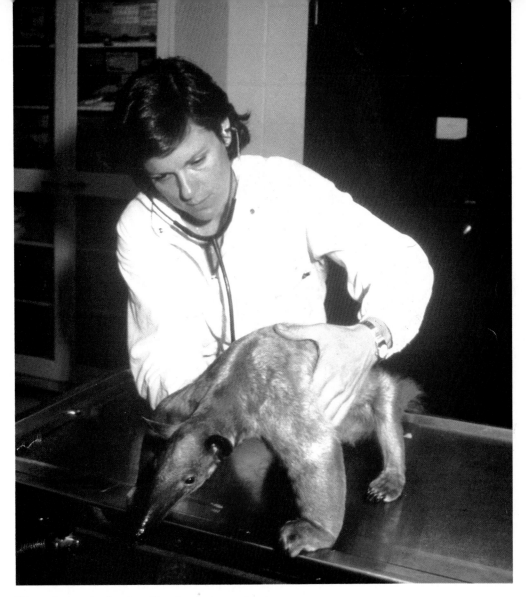

This vet checks the health of a baby anteater.

The doctor feels for bumps and broken bones. Sometimes an X ray is needed.

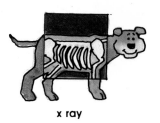

x ray

With a stethoscope doctors can listen to the heartbeat
and breathing of a chimpanzee (above) and a dog (below).

Instruments can help the doctor find out what is wrong. A thermometer tells the body temperature. With a stethoscope, heart and lungs can be listened to. A microscope shows the doctor what kind of germs an animal has.

stethoscope

thermometer

microscope

germs

examining room

An animal doctor who treats small animals has them brought to his office. The doctor sees his patients in an examining room. It has a table, a sink, and a cabinet for medicine. This room is kept very clean.

The doctor has many helpers. A nurse helps

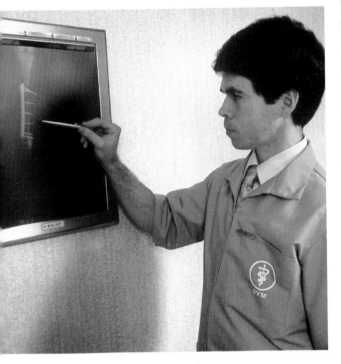

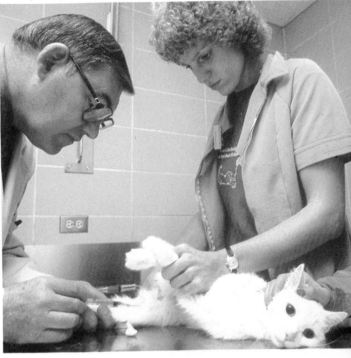

X rays (left) are used to check inside an animal's body. A lab assistant (above) holds a cat still while the vet gives it a shot.

lab assistant

the doctor examine the patients. A lab assistant may take blood tests and X rays.

blood test

13

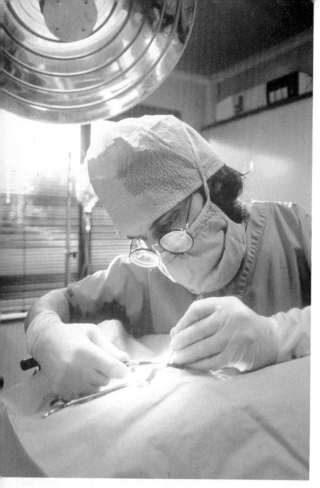

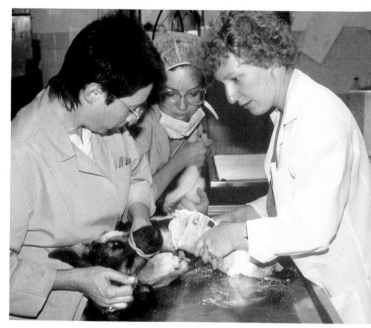

Eye surgery on a dog (left) takes special skill. A vet and her assistants (above) remove a cast from a dog. The dog's mouth is tied to prevent it from biting the hands that help it. To avoid causing pain, vets give animals a gas (below) that puts them to sleep before an operation.

Animals need surgeons just as people do. A surgeon does everything from fixing bones to helping baby animals be born. A surgeon works in an operating room.

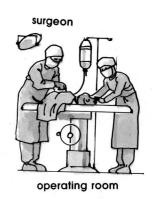

surgeon

operating room

When an animal is very sick or has surgery, it stays in the animal hospital. There the doctor and helpers care for it.

If cages are not kept clean, other illnesses can develop.

cages

The hospital rooms for animals are cages. Everything is kept clean. There is always fresh water for the patients.

Most animals need shots to keep them from getting sick. They also need a special shot for rabies to keep them from getting that disease. If they have rabies and bite someone, that person may need shots, too.

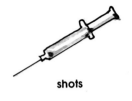

shots

When animals get toothaches, the doctor pulls their teeth or fills their cavities.

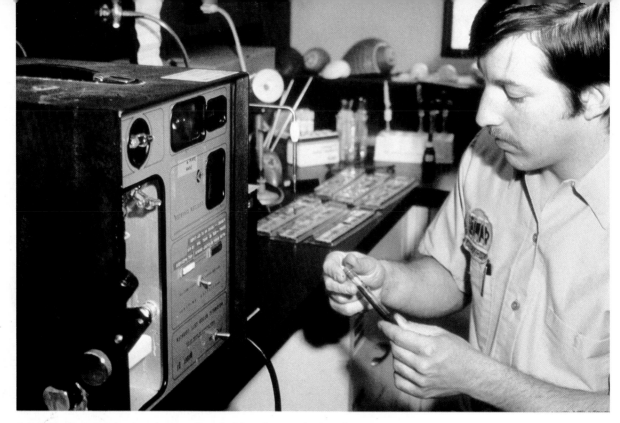

A lab technician looks at an animal's blood sample for disease.

laboratory

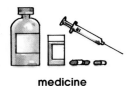

medicine

Some doctors work with animals in a laboratory, or lab. They find out what makes animals get sick. They make new medicines to help animals get well.

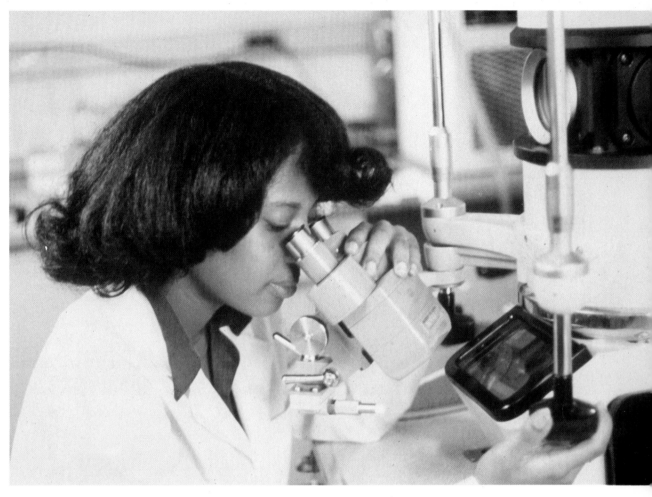

Microscopes are used to do research on animal diseases.

They learn how to keep diseases from spreading. This is called research. What these doctors learn will help all other doctors.

research

Often a squeeze shoot (left) is used to hold cattle still for shots. Another kind of instrument (right) is used to hold open the mouth of a pig.

There are large-animal doctors who often live in, or near, the country. They take care of cows, horses, sheep, and other big farm animals.

A plunger device is used to get a pill down a steer's throat.

It is hard to give pills to
large animals. The doctor
uses a plunger with a
long handle to get the
pill down the throat of a
large animal without
hurting it.

Whether they are large or small, city dwellers or country cousins,
animals need veterinarians to help them stay healthy.

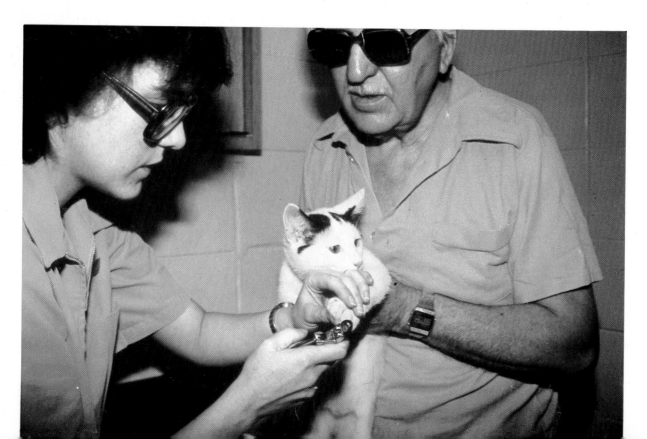

animal hospital

There are many special jobs that animal doctors do. They may work full time on a large ranch. Some work in large city animal hospitals. Sometimes they work in an emergency room on animals who have had accidents.

emergency room

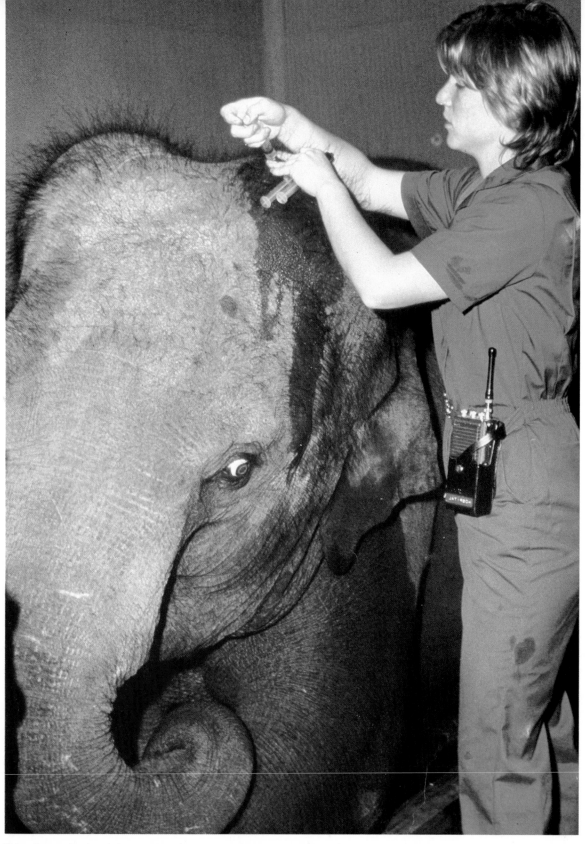

This circus doctor takes care of a sore on an elephant's head.

A large circus keeps an animal doctor at all times to care for the animals under the "Big Top."

There is an animal
doctor at every race
track to look after the
horses. A famous race
horse may even have its
own doctor.

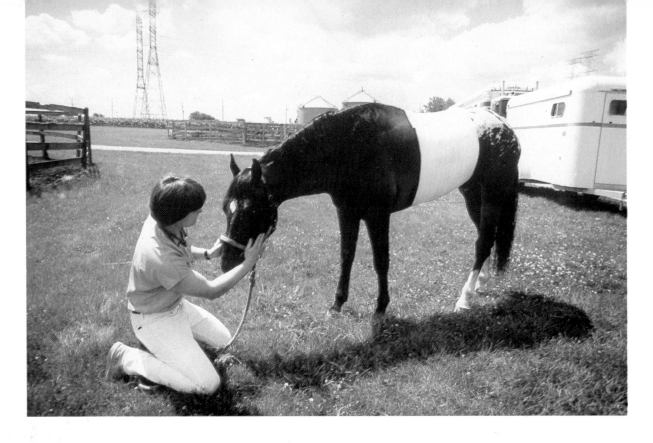

Some veterinarians work only with horses.

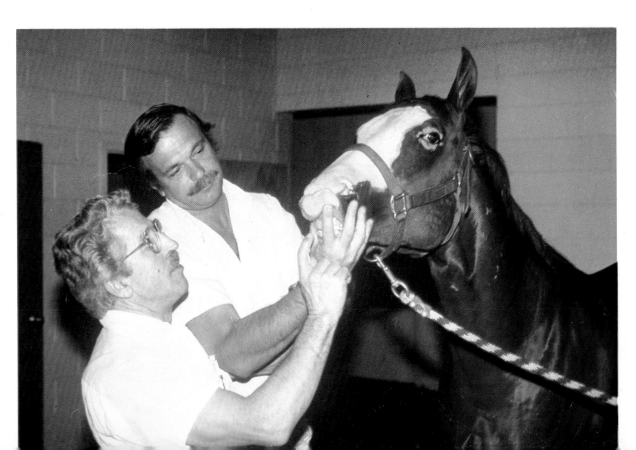

To prevent some kinds of sickness, vets will give animals special medicine.

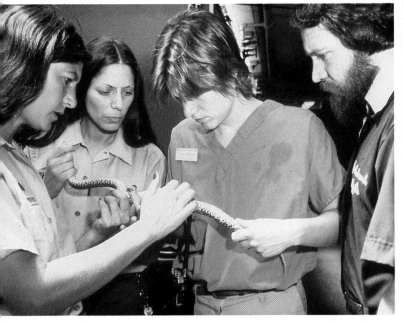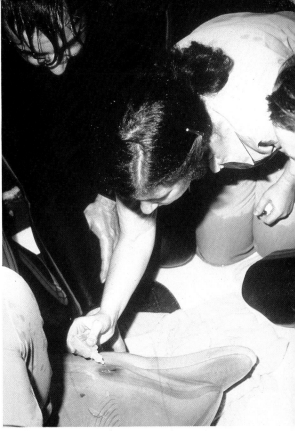

Like all animals, snakes (left) and porpoises (right) must
depend on doctors to take care of them when they are sick.

The animal doctor is a
friend to animals and to
humans. If you love
animals and work hard
to learn how to take care
of them, you can be an
animal doctor.

WORDS YOU SHOULD KNOW

coat (KOAT)—an animal's fur or hair

disease (diz • EEZ)—a sickness or illness

examining room (ig • ZAM • uh • ning ROOM)—the room where a doctor sees, or examines, patients

laboratory (LAB • uh • ruh • tor • ee)—a place where doctors or other scientists do experiments or other tests

microscope (MI • kruh • skohp)—an instrument that makes tiny things look large

patients (PAY • shunts)—persons or animals being cared for by a doctor

rabies (RAY • beez)—a disease animals usually receive from the bite of another animal; it can be passed on to humans

research (rih • SURCH)—study and experiments that look for new facts, new medicines, etc.

stethoscope (STETH • uh • skohp)—an instrument doctors use to listen to the heart and lungs

surgeon (SIR • juhn)—a doctor who operates on patients to cure them

thermometer (thir • MOM • uht • er)—an instrument doctors use to take a patient's body temperature

veterinarian (vet • uh • run • AIR • ee • un)—a doctor who cares for animals that are sick or hurt

X ray (EKS RAY)—a picture of the inside of a part of the body

INDEX

PHOTO CREDITS

Hillstrom Stock Photo:
© Norma Morrison—Cover, 6, 22 (bottom), 28 (top)
© Brooks & Vankirk—13 (right)
© Ray F. Hillstrom—27 (2 photos)

Journalism Services—4, 8, 10 (bottom), 13 (left)
© Paul E. Burd—20 (left)
© Susan Reich—9, 10 (top), 18, 24, 29 (left)

Image Finders:
© R. Flanagan—14 (top right), 14 (bottom), 16

EKM-Nepenthe:
© Robert V. Eckert Jr.—14 (top left)

Tom Stack & Associates:
© Warren D. Colman—19

USDA—20 (right), 21, 22 (top), 28 (bottom)

Nawrocki Stock Photo:
© Ken Sexton—29 (right)

About the Author

Kay Lumley is a nationally known reading specialist, and author of numerous books and articles on reading and its teaching. She is a graduate of Lock Haven State College (Pa.) and the Pennsylvania State University. Her experience includes teaching and supervision at all levels from elementary through university classes, and director of The Reading Center for the Washington, D.C. Public Schools. Mrs. Lumley is a member of the Reading Is Fundamental (RIF) board of directors. She is a trustee of the Williamsport Area Community College, Williamsport, Pa., and is an active participant in leading professional and civic associations. She lives near her son, Joe, in Rauchtown, Pa. with many assorted animal friends.